"THINGS I HEARD MY PROFESSOR SAY"

INSIGHTS FROM MY FAVORITE BUSINESS SCHOOL CLASS

D1366991

Curtis L. Odom, Ed.D.
With Eli Boulous

BOOK•NOL•O•GY
n. delivering useable information and knowledge
that adds value to people's lives

AN IMPRINT FROM ADDUCENT

To Our Success!

[signature]

Jay,

I hope you find the wisdom & insights in this book uplifting & inspiring as you continue on your path towards "success" & whatever that looks like for you!

To Our Success,

[signature]

"THINGS I HEARD MY PROFESSOR SAY"

INSIGHTS FROM MY FAVORITE BUSINESS SCHOOL CLASS

Curtis L. Odom, Ed.D.
With Eli Boulous

Things I Heard My Professor Say

Curtis L. Odom, Ed.D.
With Eli Boulous

ISBN (paperback) 9781937592967

Published by Booknology
(A Business & Educational Imprint from Adducent)
www.AdducentCreative.com
Jacksonville, Florida USA
Published in the United States of America

All statements of fact, opinion, or analysis expressed are those of the author and do not reflect the official positions or views of the publisher. Nothing in the contents should be construed as asserting or implying authentication of information or endorsement of the author's views. This book and subjects discussed herein are designed to provide the author's opinion on the subject matter covered and is for informational purposes only.

Thank you, Eli for your priceless gift of the proof of my impact.

DEDICATION

To my late professor, dissertation chair, coach, mentor, friend, and professorial role model, Dr. John 'Jack' Mc-Manus. Your steady support and unyielding belief in me through four years of earning my doctorate from Pepperdine University were invaluable.

Thank you for encouraging me to dare to achieve my audacious goal of becoming full-time faculty at a business school in Boston. Your teaching me to "pay it forward" became my life mantra. And my life mantra has allowed me to discover that my purpose is to inspire students with my personal experience as proof of what can happen when you live a life with gratutude as your attitude. The power of your example will be with me forever.

To Strive, To Seek, To Find, and Not To Yield – Tennyson

ACKNOWLEDGMENTS

To my amazing wife and best friend for life, Nelia. I will never forget that there is no me without you. This book, my fifth, being written during a global pandemic adds yet another chapter to our incredible story. Your willingness to always listen to me talk out my ideas and aspirations as my thinking partner continues to be a blessing. I cannot imagine my life without you by my side to share every moment. Thank you for your undying support. I love you!

To my lovely daughter and best giggle buddy, Alyssa. I've watched you grow from an adorable little girl into a charming and lovely young woman. It is a blessing and a privilege to be your father. I aspire daily to be your hero, and your role model for how to live a grateful life. The greatest joys of my life have been moments spent sitting next to you on a beach at sunset. I love you!

ACKNOWLEDGMENTS

FOREWORD

*"If I say something twice, then it's important.
Write it down."*

Quite the wake-up at 9:30 on a brisk Boston morning during the first Friday of the semester. In front of me stood Dr. Curtis Odom, red socks donned, cufflinks glimmering, purple bow tie expertly knotted. You can imagine one's indifference as a final-semester senior in a required class, but this man had a commanding presence, a personality that filled the room, and an aura about him that said: "You should listen to what I'm about to tell you."

So, I grabbed a pen.

Imagine you're 22, on the verge of entering the "real-world" without a job lined up, and here's a professor discussing how to get a job and EXCEL at it. You would write down his words too. Dr. Odom's tales of grit, perseverance, and self-empowerment could be their own story. Yet, this book, compiled from his words in an Organizational Behavior course, is for all of us looking for a job, wanting to improve our current situation (personally and professionally) and to seize the next step in our lives.

Years have passed since my time as Dr. Odom's student, yet two memories still stand out. On the first day of class, he taught us about the "game" being played at every company, seeing it, and succeeding in it. After working at four different firms, I knew exactly what he was talking about. Yet, no one ever said it explicitly, even in my four years of business school. In my final year, I learned the most important lessons of my college career in the first 20 minutes of his class.

Later that semester, I paid him a visit to share post-college plans and thoughts. He didn't tell me what job to pursue. He didn't tell me what salary to aim for. He didn't even tell me which website to use. Instead, in classic Odom-fashion, he shared a pearl of wisdom that jump-started my professional career. He told me: "Write down five things you'd like to do day-to-day. Search for them together online and see where it takes you." With this, Dr. Odom gave me something greater than a list of instructions. He gave me the tools to help me succeed. Most importantly, he gave me a template I could use to help others. And therein lies one of Dr. Curtis Odom's greatest qualities, his altruism.

What's most impressive about Dr. Odom is not his accolades or achievements; it's his commitment to Paying It Forward—his passion for creating the next generation of leaders. He shares his wisdom and experiences to empower people like you and me to live our best lives. The fact that a former student is writing this foreword is a testament to this ideal and a testament to Dr. Odom's dedication to his student's success.

As you read the exact words I heard my professor say, I challenge you to reflect and think about how they can help you. I have and will continue to use this book's wisdom to create the life I want to live and position myself for success based on the hand I'm dealt. His words have inspired countless others to be the people they want to be; now it's time for you to experience them yourself. It is my great privilege to introduce Dr. Curtis Odom!

- Eli Boulous, 1/28/2021

PREFACE

I am full-time faculty in the D'Amore-McKim School of Business at Northeastern University in Boston. I enjoy teaching a class that I designed and developed entitled Management Consulting in Organizations which has become quite popular on campus. This project-based class is a capstone course for the undergraduate Business Degree. It is also one of the two required courses for the recently created Consulting minor.

Prior to being a professor, I graduated high school and began a ten-year career in the United States Navy, including having the opportunity to serve in Operation Desert Storm. When I joined the Navy, I did not know what I wanted to do with my life. I did know that I wanted to travel and see the world. The Navy taught me many things during my time in uniform. One of the many things is that it is okay not to know what you want to do – it is more important to know what you do NOT want to do. Another thing that the Navy taught me is that if you want something, you have to go get it. No one is going to give you anything. You cannot just sit around and hope or expect opportunities. The Navy also taught me is that success is personal. I think if you allow others to tell you what success looks like; you are going to end up disappointing yourself trying to achieve something defined by someone else. If success to you is getting up each day and making your bed, then count that as a personal success! Ultimately, the Navy taught me that leadership is all about connecting with people. If you cannot connect with people, you cannot lead. People want to be led by those that they have a connection with, by those that they have something in common with, by people that they like genuinely as a person.

I got out of the Navy in 2000, moved to Detroit for an employment opportunity which led to my starting my first business as a consulting firm founded with two partners. The three of us did some good work together while having fun. I ended up selling that firm in 2003, and moved back to the East Coast to start a family with my wife. After arriving in Massachusetts, I began what would be an 11-year journey of working for many different companies while growing my knowledge, skill, and ability with each opportunity. I stayed at each place just long enough to learn as much as I needed to climb higher with the next opportunity.

Thinking deeply in 2004 on what I had learned while in the Navy, I felt compelled to claim what would be my career. In that moment I spoke into being that I wanted to be full-time faculty in a business school in Boston, and retire as a professor. I was not specific as to which business school – I was however specific that Boston was to be my destination.

By any measure, this would be a lofty goal to achieve – made even more audacious for someone who barely graduated high school. As a kid who grew up in Providence, Rhode Island, Boston was the first big city I had ever visited. With this goal now set, I knew that to be full-time faculty in a business school, I was going to need to earn a doctorate from an impressive school. And that meant graduating from a "one word name" school. Because one word named schools impress people – Harvard, Yale, Stanford, Dartmouth, Columbia, and so forth. There was no other way around it. So, I took the opportunity to apply to the only two programs at one word named schools the time that would allow me to continue to work full-time while earning my doctorate. My daughter had just been born which meant that I needed to continue working to support my family while pursuing such an involved academic achievement. At that time, only two schools presented an opportunity of attending respected university through a blended program while working full-time – Penn (University of Pennsylvania) in Philadelphia, and Pepperdine in Malibu.

I dove into researching these two amazing options. Did I want to spend over $100,000 to go to school in rainy and cold Philadelphia, or for that same investment finally visit California and take classes overlooking the Pacific Ocean in sunny and warm Malibu? Painfully undecided, I applied to both universities and was accepted by both. How did I ultimately decide where to go? I listened to Horace Greely who was purported to have said,

"Go West, young man, go West. There is health in the country, and room away from our crowds of idlers and imbeciles."

So, off to Malibu where I would get my Doctorate in Education from Pepperdine graduating Summa Cum Laude, Phi Delta Kappa in 2009 while having worked full-time. I had completed the first major step in the pursuit of being a business school professor. But my journey was far from over. What followed next was six years of taking different adjunct professor gigs to build my teaching resume, grow my knowledge of pedagogy in practice, and create my professional network within academia.

In the spring of 2016, I got the unexpected opportunity to apply for a Visiting Lecturer role at Northeastern to begin teaching full-time that fall semester. Later, after two years of proving myself as a Visiting Professor, I was offered the opportunity to apply for a newly created full-time faculty position of Assistant Teaching Professor – a non-tenure track position externally titled Executive Professor. The goal I set for myself in 2004 had become my reality 16 years later through persistent learning, and continued growth. I was about to become full-time faculty in a business school in Boston. Audacious goal achieved!

Since that moment, my favorite days are always ones where I get to teach and learn at the same time. I do not profess to know everything. I just happen to know a lot about a few things which makes me open to learn about things that I have never even heard of before. That to me makes learning fun! My having a growth mindset allows me to have an unshakably optimistic outlook which contributes to me having gratitude as my only attitude.

When I am in my role of professor on campus, I bring my 20 plus years of knowledge, skills, ability, and experiences together to create a learning culture in the classroom. Every semester I create an "organization" with my students in which they learn content by having it placed into real-life context. Each class, like every organization, is made up of people who have different preferences for how they like to work and learn while honoring the wealth of diverse experiences that they bring along with them. It makes sense to try to understand those preferences, not from a standpoint of how we are different, but more importantly how much we are very similar. In my classroom, I encourage the practice that we are all learning from each other in a safe environment for purposeful discovery.

Embracing those unique similarities with my students, we then enter a place where the classroom culture provides the four things that I talk about each of us wanting from anywhere we spend our time, whether for work or play. When you walk into my classroom as a student, or into an organization as an employee – you have four non-negotiable wants:

IV

1. You want <u>to be welcomed</u>. Meaning that you are greeted with respect and genuine appreciation for you as a person.

2. You want <u>to feel valued</u>, that people enjoy your presence, your knowledge, and skills because they add value to the organization.

3. You want <u>to contribute</u> in a way that allows you to showcase your abilities and experiences and be rewarded either intrinsically or extrinsically for those contributions.

4. Most importantly, you want <u>to be your authentic self</u> while doing the work that you do. That however you choose to identify yourself, is not just tolerated, but embraced and celebrated.

And that last want is the most important one that many leaders in business still have trouble accepting – that younger generations have absolutely no problem with being their authentic self in the workplace. They will not ask permission to show up in their truth. And they will not stay around long mentally or physically in a place that they cannot be 100% themselves.

As a validating example, each semester I look at the engagement of my students. Each semester I have over 100 students that I believe all show up as their authentic self. And it was great to meet every single one of them as who they were, and as they chose to introduce themselves. Everything we learn in life we learn from someone else! *including other life forms*

Often during my corporate career, I put myself in situations where I could not be my authentic self, and needed to suppress the real me to remain employed. Finally, in 2011, I said no more! I swore that I would never again try to be someone that I am not –I would forever more be who I was meant to be. And if I ever found myself again in a place where I could not be myself, I would depart to find another place to be. I would keep looking for career opportunities until I found a place where I did not have to pretend to be someone I wasn't to work there.

Having accomplished so many goals to be here now in my life, I relish being a professor and the opportunity of paying it forward. Nothing excites me more than to engage bright minds in dialogue and spirited conversation in a college classroom. It is exciting being a professor because you are constantly surrounded by smart, young people. And it is in this way that your mind stays sharp, and you get the chance every day to build your legacy.

It took me many years to realize that the only place I could EVER totally be myself would be as my own boss – which is where I find myself now running my own management consulting firm when not teaching, and teaching from my lived experience as a professional when I am in the classroom. One of the many things I have learned in life from business is that stress is defined as going too long trying to be someone that you are not, or doing something that you really do not want to do. Consequently, I no longer have any of those stresses – and I am grateful that I get to be my authentic self without ever again having to ask for permission.

I am excited to share this book with you! What makes the writing of this book so beautifully ironic to me is that you will be reading the career learnings and lessons of someone who barely made it out of high school but who found their personal definition of success as a business owner, and full-time faculty member at a top business school in Boston.

In the following pages you will find over 20 years of professional insights, lessons learned, and personal experiences as captured by a student in my class who gave me the greatest gift of my career – a transcript of me putting my entire career's worth of context into the content of academic lectures taught over a fall semester in a college classroom.

- Curtis L. Odom, Ed.D.

INTRODUCTION

It was the first Tuesday of the Fall semester of 2018. I was scheduled to teach a 10:00am class in Organizational Behavior that was required for undergraduate business majors. As such, you could have students in the class from any class year. Most were in their second or third year, but there were always a handful of students who had just gotten around to this course in their final semester. Why? Maybe because the idea of a required class doesn't sound all that appealing. Or because since the course is offered every semester in multiple sections, there is no urgency to take it as soon as possible or during the recommended second year of school.

What is Organizational Behavior you ask? It is a course that is a mix of Psychology, Sociology, and Anthropology designed to help students understand the groups and organizations to which they currently belong, and with which you will become involved in your future career. Wherever we go, we are surrounded by organizations. Most of us are born into a family which is our first organization. We then spend the vast majority of our lives working in and for organizations for our profession, and we even die as part of an organization that we helped create known as our immediate family. The goal of the Organizational Behavior course is to build a student's awareness and understanding of individual, interpersonal, and group behavior in organizations and the subsequent impact on organizational events in our own lives.

This was my custom at the time, teaching three classes on Tuesdays and Fridays. One class in the morning and two classes in the afternoon. But the students in this particular required morning class offering made it my favorite class to teach that semester. Why? Because this group of students got it! They were unlike the usual students in a required class – they were beyond engaged. They wanted to be there, they were eager to learn, and their amount of class participation was through the roof. Now I would like to say it was because I was so engaging as their professor, but I think instead think that their engagement was because the course content was put into such context that they could not get enough of my making connections to their learning.

In the classroom of today, it is not strange at all to see students with their laptops, tablets, or smartphones being used to take notes during class time instead of paper notebooks. Some students have bought the e-book version of the textbook, and sure some are on Snapchat. But it doesn't bother me like it does some of my professor colleagues for three reasons. First, because I never forget what it is like to be a student. Second, because whatever I say in class is fair game for them on the midterm and final exams – if they don't pay attention it is their loss. And third, because if my class if that boring to my students then I deserve to have them be disengaged. Luckily for me, I have never had the latter said about me or my style of teaching. Why? Because in each class we would review a variety of concepts that explain the structure, processes and outcomes of example organizations and apply them to real world current events, my professional background, and their co-op experience as ways to put things into context.

My conversational style of teaching is to gain an awareness of the opportunities and challenges facing individuals and groups in organizational settings and teams. I give them the safe space to develop essential skills needed to self-reflect and assess their own behavior and the behavior of others in organizational settings and in teams. I want them to build confidence in sharing ideas, exploring issues and making new discoveries in a group setting. But most importantly, I encourage them to recognize and build an appreciation of individual differences of members of the class and individual team members. What I ask of my students is that they arrive on time to each class prepared. That means not only having read the assigned material, but ready to actively engage in our classroom discussion.

I take the opportunity of being a professor as an honor. To be called professor is something that I cherish. As such, I see it as my priority to make the course and the material as understandable, interesting, and relevant as possible to each student. I strive during every session to create an open environment in which every member of the class feels comfortable sharing their thoughts, ideas, and their authentic identity. And from creating this environment of mutual respect and expectation of hearing content put into context in each class is how I arrived at the content for this book. One engaged student from this particular class, Eli Boulous captured this moment by noting the insights he heard as the things that I, as his professor said that most impacted him from his moments spent this required class.

One of my most cherished gifts as a professor came as an unexpected email from one of my most memorable students:

Mon 12/10/2018 5:37 PM

Hi Professor Odom,

I hope this email finds you well on your travels. My apologies again for missing our meeting last week, I am still kicking myself over it.

I wanted to thank you again for the incredible semester. It was by far my favorite and most impactful class since coming to Northeastern! I thank you for your dedication to both your craft and your students.

Because your class was so helpful, I found it beneficial to capture your insights and categorize them for maximum applicability. Please see the attached playbook!

Wishing you and your family a happy holiday season and new year! I look forward to our paths crossing again one day in the near future.

To Our Success!

Eli Boulous

THINGS I HEARD
MY PROFESSOR SAY

There are four things people want
from a job:

To be welcomed.
To be valued.
To be able to contribute.
To be their authentic self.

Having a healthy working relationship with a colleague doesn't require having a close friendship.

Influencers share thoughts with decision makers.

But it is the decision maker that you must impress.

Your personality will either be in line or out of line with a company culture.

Stay anywhere that you can be truly be who you want to be.

Stress comes from spending too much time trying to be someone you're not, or doing something you really don't want to be doing.

Personality lends itself to presence.

How you come across to others creates
what people say and think about you.

People are not a company's competitive differentiator.

How a company treats its people is what truly differentiates the company.

Inclusion lives inside of the organization and is tied to culture.

Without failure, and learning from that failure, there can be no innovation.

Organizations change for one of two reasons: Either because they want to or because they have to.

Being entrepreneurial doesn't mean creating something from nothing.

It can also mean improving a current task, product or process.

A learning organization is about being flexible and survivable.

Resistance to change kills more growth and innovation opportunities than you can even imagine.

The better that a company does, the more change-resistant it becomes.

'If it ain't broke, don't fix it' only worked in the industrial age.

Organizations have long memories.

What the culture remembers about someone often outlives their working for the organization.

Employer Value Proposition:

What you think it would be like to work there.

Employee Experience:

What it's actually like for you
to work there.

Be either the first person in the office or the last, but *never* both.

You get no credit for being first in the office, but you often get credit for being there last.

Your boss should always be shown respect due to their positional power.

But that doesn't mean that you have to like your boss as a person.

Leaders are conveyors of corporate culture.

To say that we need culture change is to say that we need our leaders to think, speak, and act differently.

How we do business is just as important as the what of the business that we do.

Good practices lead to good business results.

Many organizations don't have a view of their current state, which is critical to setting goals to achieve their desired future state.

Consistently update your mindset, skillset, and toolset as the way to increase your value to an organization and increase your career opportunities.

Staying at one company should mean that you continually received new opportunities for growth, not from being afraid to find new opportunities elsewhere.

There is no change without a sense of urgency. There are many things that, while important, do not drive change.

Only something seen as an imperative can move someone to take action.

The true character and integrity of a person will be revealed during moments of adversity.

People and organizations enter a state of mental transition and potentially begin to grieve the moment they hear things will change.

Keep counsel at home!

The colleague you commiserate with today could become your rival for an opportunity later with a transcript of your thoughts and words to use against you.

Absence/presence of emotion drives
problems/success in business.

The longer that you let task or process conflict go, the more likely it will become relationship conflict.

Groups thrive on cooperation while teams thrive on collaboration.

Conformity is an aspect of compliance.

Conformity lies in silence.

Cross functional teams are best at achieving results as most business problems are multidimensional and highly complex in nature.

Those who avoid conflict choose to not to use the tools of effective communication.

Personal biases are a barrier to effective communication.

If you can't communicate with someone, maybe you should change the way (how) you are communicating.

Leaders look for the best way to communicate with each of their people.

Communication is not a one size fits all task.

The greatest threat to an organization is a class action lawsuit.

It is for this reason that compliance training is a necessary evil.

The best organizations plan for change – the worst organizations hastily react to change as it happens.

Centers of influence are the people in an organization who exemplify the company culture and lead by their example how to get work done within the culture.

Look for power brokers and notice with whom they associate.

It is much more important who knows you, *not* who you know, that builds your professional brand.

Emotional Intelligence is understanding that the best intent can yield a most unintended impact.

Look for patterns of behavior as they shape people's perception of you.

How you are perceived becomes your professional brand.

Positive feedback reinforces good behavior; the absence of feedback encourages bad behavior.

The three P's of decision making
require the asking of:

What is Plausible?
What is Possible?
What is Probable?

The three most used tools in an effective leader's toolbox are inspiration, influence, and persuasion.

Leadership is about connecting with people.

You *lead* people –
but you *manage* things.

Learn how to do both well
if you want to succeed.

Customers buy from people,
not companies.

Influence and inspiration don't require an introduction.

Appeal to three things for motivation
and employee engagement:

Head
Heart
Wallet

You won't truly know what culture an organization has until you run afoul of that culture.

Around six months is when the organization's culture will reveal itself, because that is the maximum length of time that someone can be on their best behavior.

Always communicate to express,
and never to impress.

Let people know what you're expecting from them in the email subject line.

Never use email to the take place of an in-person conversation.

Some leaders don't realize that their job would be easier if they actually took time to connect on a personal level with the people they are leading.

Positive feedback given at wrong time
can be negative.

Practice the four pillars of communication:

Nonverbal
Thinking
Speaking
Listening

Where is your mind when you speak with someone?

If it cannot be on the conversation at hand, reschedule the meeting.

Always check twice with your boss to get agreement on what a good job will look like before beginning any newly assigned task.

Starting with "In my experience"
can't be challenged.

No one can tell you didn't have a life
or career experience. But they can
(and will) challenge your research,
your thinking, and your feelings if you
disagree with them.

Your career success depends on having advocates.

What is an advocate?

A person of influence who will say good things about you and your abilities when you are not around to hear them at a critical moment.

Leadership at the highest is level is thinking about the success of the business as a whole, in the order of the business first, of the team second, and of yourself last.

No boss likes to be blindsided by bad news. Ever!

The best leaders know who their critical
employees are and do all they can do
to show them that they are valued and
appreciated.

Just saying 'Thank You' isn't enough.

Leaders are always on stage and being viewed (and critiqued) from every angle under the brightest lights of public opinion.

Good leaders will always ask how they can help you.

They ask: "How are we going to do this together? How do we all win?"

The only leadership style that works is a flexible one.

Having a rigid leadership style will make you ineffective. You should not attempt to lead each of your people the same way.

Leading up: Communicate how you need to be led and ask for feedback.

Only feedback can close our blind spots.

Only by receiving both constructive and confirming feedback can our personal and professional growth occur.

There can be no abuse of power without first there being a dependency.

What or who you depend upon has power over you. Therefore, learn how to depend on yourself.

The key to successful leadership is influence, not authority.

While you can *tell* someone do something, it is always better to have your actions or example *compel* someone to act.

You can't play the corporate if you don't know the game exists, if you don't know the rules, or if no one is willing to teach you how to play.

In your first 90 days of a new position or with a new organization, your primary job is to look, listen, and learn.

No matter what you do for work, you were hired to get results.

Never forget that you only get to keep your job by getting measurable results.

The best leaders create an environment where people are motivated and engaged to do their absolute best, to get the results that they are paid to get.

Expert is the only title that you have but cannot give yourself.

You do not get to call yourself an expert – unless you are fine with your doing so exposing you to be a pompous ass.

The little things you do or don't do will impact how, and if, you move forward in a job interview.

Intensity, persistence, and direction
are wasted without being part of a plan
attached to a *goal*.

Employee engagement has a direct line to customer satisfaction.

Happy employees create happy customers, and happy customers leads to customer retention.

The most important business relationship you can have is with your boss. Your success and growth will flow through that relationship.

Even if they are a bad boss, you will learn from them how *not* to lead when you get the chance.

The mark of an empowering leader is one who will tell you what needs to be done, when it needs to be done, where it needs to be done, and why it needs to be done.

They will never tell you *how* it needs to be done.

If you don't *ask* for what you want, don't be surprised by what you don't *get*.

Don't be disappointed by not achieving results that you didn't put in the work to get.

Just because the *company* hired you does not mean that your *boss* wanted to hire you.

Every six months you should be able to show through your results where you have added value to the organization by making the company money, or saving the company money.

Period.

Quickest way to get promoted is to prove your ability to get results with each opportunity is to do work at the next higher level.

If you can't be replaced,
you can't be promoted.

True leaders realize that *your* success ensures *their* success.

If you are not willing to lose everything for something, then you cannot truly win at anything.

You shouldn't work to live up to someone else's definition of success.

Find and pursue your own version of success.

The Rubicon: The point in business or any endeavor that you reach when it's further to go back to start than it is to go forward and achieve your goal.

Breakeven Point: When you start providing value and getting results for the organization that justifies the salary that the company is paying you.

You can be born with leadership traits, but leadership skills come from trial and error, success and failure, time and experience.

If you don't learn how to fail, you won't know how to appreciate success when it arrives.

It's not important where you start your journey or where you go, but if you can allow yourself to enjoy the journey.

Your time is the greatest resource and the one thing you can't get back. None of us knows how much time we have left, but we all know that none of us will be given any more time.

Relentlessly practice the 5R's of being in the Right place, at the Right time, with the Right message, with the Right preparation, and always with the Right attitude.

The legacy of leadership is not in leading, but in paying it forward in the helping to create other leaders.

Networking is equal parts give and take – walk into each opportunity ready to ask three questions, and ready to make three statements you think will benefit the other person.

There are key phases in every business relationship that cannot be rushed or forced – relationships are based on first being known, second being liked, and third being trusted, *before* ever being referred or hired or mentored.

Compensation is payment for your time and your talent.

There are only two ways to increase your compensation: by either increasing your time spent or raising the value of your (knowledge, skills, abilities, and results) talent.

Most negotiations fail because of
inflexibility.

Everyone is coming to the meeting
with an agenda. So be ready to give
something order to get anything.

Negotiating goes on both overtly
and covertly.

If you do not know that you are
constantly negotiating, then you have
already lost.

The first person to talk about money in any negotiation loses!

Everything is negotiable if the respect is mutual.

You will have to be selfish with your time as you go about growing your success.

Market your adaptability to change.

Business is about evolution, and to survive, companies need to learn how to be agile – which means they will need to hire people who have demonstrated an ability to be agile.

Minimize your use of "What" questions and more often use "How, Why, and When" questions as you onboard into a new organization.

"What" questions do not tell you about the culture, only what was done in the past.

Networking Elevator Pitch:

Who you are.
What do you do.
How you are different than anyone else
who does that.
How you would help the company smart
enough to hire you.

Don't get so busy building your professional career that you forget to make a personal life.

When your authentic self doesn't fit with a company culture, you have only two choices – either stay and conform to what you feel is wrong or depart for what you feel is right.

Ask: Do you feel like you're learning something?

If not, then it may be time to go.

Most people listen with the intent to reply, not with the intent to understand. Others only sit quietly waiting for you to stop talking.

Sometimes the best thing to do in a situation is nothing at all. Especially when your initial reaction to an ask or a presented opportunity does not illicit a "Hell yes!" as your response.

You don't always get to pick when and where you will be asked to become a leader.

You can't outrun Mother Nature or Father Time – so live a full life that you can be proud of while you can.

Live a life so full that your story is a source of inspiration to others long after your death.

Leaders create culture change by changing themselves.

Personal and professional support networks are invaluable; no one succeeds on their own.

Prioritize your life and business in a way that lines up with what you personally value most.

It is easy to want something, but being willing to do what it takes to get it is hard.

People always talk about giving back as some obligatory form of payment for your having had success.

Instead, think of giving back as paying it forward by leaving a legacy of opportunity for the success of someone else.

ABOUT THE AUTHOR

Dr. Curtis Odom is an Executive Professor of Management in the D'Amore-McKim School of Business at Northeastern University.

Educated as a scholar-practitioner, Dr. Odom's experiences as a management consultant inform both his research, and teaching philosophy. Curtis believes that learning should be experiential and participant-centered and seeks to motivate, inspire, and instill in his students a sense of ownership of their learning journey. His ability to connect academic content to workplace and workforce context is born of a 20-year industry career as a corporate executive, entrepreneur, management consultant, and executive coach.

Away from Northeastern, Curtis is an experienced entrepreneur, business owner, and former Fortune 100 executive who consults, coaches, mentors, and teaches from his experience of getting results. His clients hire him for his depth of business knowledge to motivate, educate and inspire aspiring and current entrepreneurs to achieve a higher level of success, professionally and personally. Curtis aligns business owners actions to their vision for their organization, supports them in the execution of key strategies and tactics to move initiatives forward, and helps them gain critical knowledge necessary for their business and personal success.

Curtis is an international award-winning business transformation executive, and acclaimed management consultant who provides pragmatic advice, coaching, and guidance to company executives, senior leaders, and management teams. Curtis gets results by quickly connecting the dots of an organizational culture to unlock the potential of employees, harness intellectual property and proprietary technology, and streamline internal processes to efficiently maximize company potential. Curtis adds value through his ability to step in and amplify business performance during times of leadership transition, mergers and acquisitions, process improvement, and operational optimization at critical transitional moments.

Curtis is often called to lead targeted business transformations to help iconic organizations compete both more effectively and efficiently, or make a strategic pivot. Curtis partners with his clients often during the bold, seismic shifts that an organization must make to both accelerate and execute change and strategic growth beyond typical measures or incremental advancements.

Prior to his industry and academic careers, Curtis served on active duty for 10 years in the United States Navy which included being deployed during Operation Desert Storm.